The Story of
Google

Adam Sutherland

Google apps

talk

New York

Published in 2012 by The Rosen Publishing Group, Inc.
29 East 21st Street, New York, NY 10010

Commissioning editor: Camilla Lloyd
Designer: Emma Randall
Picture researcher: Shelley Noronha

Library of Congress Cataloging-in-Publication Data

Sutherland, Adam.
The story of Google/Adam Sutherland.—1st ed.
    p. cm.—(The business of high tech)
Includes bibliographical references and index.
ISBN 978-1-4488-7041-7 (library binding)—
ISBN 978-1-4488-7092-9 (pbk.)—
ISBN 978-1-4488-7093-6 (6-pack)
1. Google (Firm)—Juvenile literature. 2. Internet industry—United States—Juvenile literature. I. Title.
HD9696.8.U64G6675 2012
338.7'6102504—dc23

2011032879

Manufactured in the United States of America

CPSIA Compliance Information: Batch #W12YA: For further information, contact Rosen Publishing, New York, New York, at 1-800-237-9932.

Picture Acknowledgements: The author and publisher would like to thank the following for allowing their pictures to be reproduced in this publication. Cover and 41: © CJG-Technology/Alamy; throughout background: RedShineStudio/ Istock; 1, 5, 12, 16 (bottom), 17, 21 (right), 21, 22-23, 24-25, 31, 32, 33, 34-35, 37, 38-39 Google; 4 Xie Zhengyi/ AP/Press Association Images; 9 Mark Blinch/Reuters/Corbis Getty Images; 11, 14-15 (top) Getty Images; 18 Karl-Josef Hildenbrand/epa/Corbis; 19 copyright and permission by Ruth Kedar; 20 Bertrand Gardel/Hemis/Corbis; 21 (left) Bloomberg via Getty Images; 26 Sipa Press/Rex Features; 28-29 Philippe Wojazer/Reuters/Corbis; 42 89 Studio/ Shutterstock; 43 Meawpong 34 05/Shutterstock. Every attempt has been made to clear copyright for this edition. Should there be any inadvertent omission please apply to the publisher for rectification.

Contents

The World Gets Googled!

Google is one of the best-known companies on the planet. Its search engine is used for two-thirds of Web searches in the United States, and 70 percent worldwide. Go to www.Google.com and type something into the search box. Google will search billions of Web pages to find the most relevant pages for your query, and usually brings you the results in less than half a second. No other search engine accesses more of the Internet or delivers more useful information.

A search engine is a Web site whose purpose is to search for other useful and informative sites when you type something into it. This can be anything and everything from "Nelson Mandela" to "cheap flights". You are then directed quickly and simply to sites that cover your area of interest. Google's skill at delivering useful, targeted search results has been the foundation of their success. But it is only part of the Google story.

What turned the company into the Internet business phenomenon it is today, was realizing they could get advertisers to pay for "sponsored" links on every single search they delivered.

▲ *The Google screen in China (www.google.cn).*

Larry Page and Sergey Brin have become world famous thanks to Google.

" The Internet makes information available. Google makes information accessible.

Hal Varian, Google's chief economist **"**

This financial windfall turned Google into an incredibly successful and powerful company. It took software giant Microsoft 15 years to reach one billion dollars in revenues. It took Google just six!

Like many successful companies, Google does not rest on its laurels. It has sought to increase its advertising revenues from searches by expanding around the world. At the same time, it has also extended its business model beyond just a search engine. YouTube and Google Maps, Street View and Google Earth are just some of the extra products and services that Google now offers. The Internet company that refined searches is now one of the world's biggest brands, and plans to get even bigger.

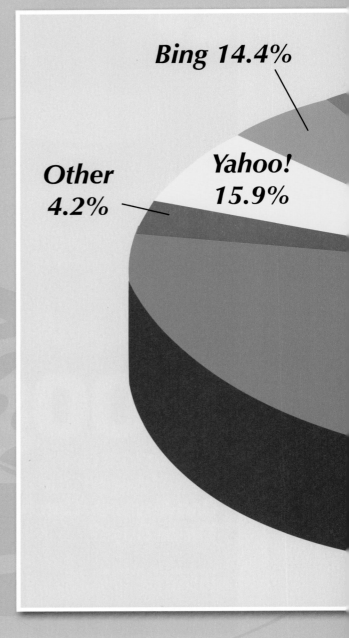

Bing 14.4%

Other 4.2%

Yahoo! 15.9%

The pie chart currently shows Google's massive dominance of the search market.

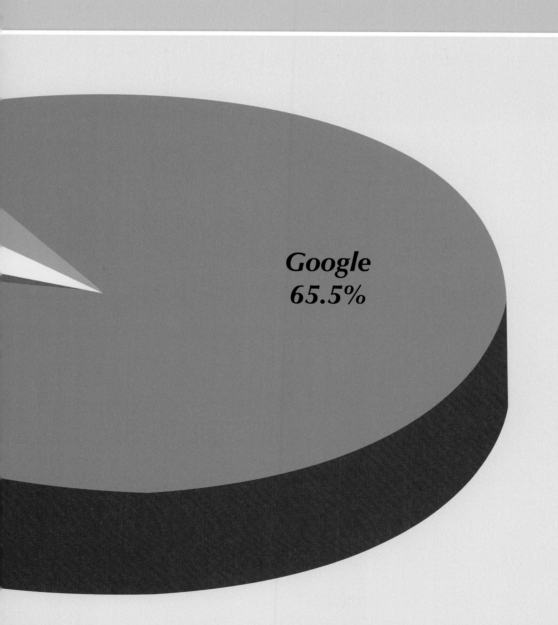

Google
65.5%

What Makes Google So Good?

The key to Google's success is the accuracy and relevance of its search. Its secret ingredient is a mathematical formula that promises to bring you only the most useful links, and even to second guess what your search actually means.

Google places links at the top of your search that have previously generated the most traffic (i.e. clicks and visits from other people). They also give higher ranking to links from reputable Web sites like CNN or the *New York Times*. By monitoring how many people click on a link, or how many other Web sites find it interesting enough to link to, Google decides whether that link is relevant and gives it a value. This value is known as PageRank, after one of Google's founders, Larry Page.

To make your search as fast as possible,

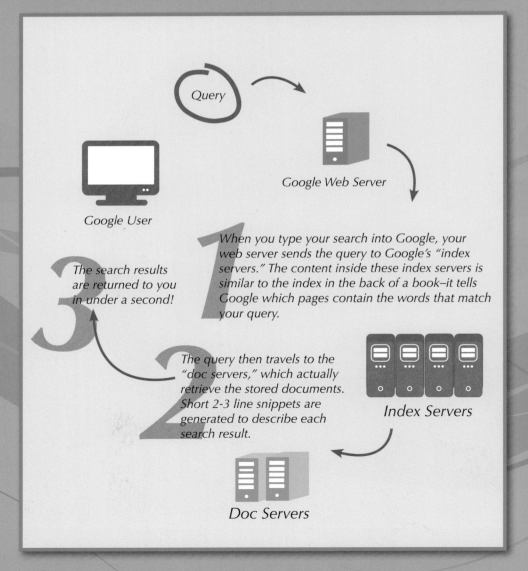

Query

Google Web Server

Google User

3 The search results are returned to you in under a second!

1 When you type your search into Google, your web server sends the query to Google's "index servers." The content inside these index servers is similar to the index in the back of a book–it tells Google which pages contain the words that match your query.

2 The query then travels to the "doc servers," which actually retrieve the stored documents. Short 2-3 line snippets are generated to describe each search result.

Index Servers

Doc Servers

▼ The black background was used by Google to support Earth Hour when people were encouraged to turn off their lights for one hour to make a statement about climate change in March 2008.

Business Matters

The Unique Selling Proposition or Point (USP) — A USP is some unique quality about a company's product or service that will attract customers to use or buy it rather than an alternative product from a competitor. When it first appeared, Google was not the only search engine that people could use, but it stood out from competitors like Excite and Yahoo! because of its functionality (what it could do), its appearance (how it looked) and its quality (how it worked).

Google has created its own copied version of the Internet. The site has scanned and ranked several billion Web pages — the figure increases daily — and stored them on its own computers, known as servers. The pages are organized by subject and every time you click "Search" hundreds of thousands of computers get to work collecting different document links and returning those links to your screen in the blink of an eye.

The search is speeded up because Google stores three copies of all its previous searches, so it doesn't have to scan the entire Web if two people ask the same question.

To help make each person's search more relevant to their personal needs, Google relies on software files called "cookies." These files live on your computer and keep track of your online activities — what search questions you ask, what Web sites you visit, how long you spend on each site, what ads you click on and what you buy online.

Because of these cookies, Google's search gets better the more you use it, as the company becomes familiar with the kind of information you are looking for.

Cookies don't identify you by name and address, but they do provide lots of valuable information on each computer's user that Google can share with advertisers.

CHAPTER 3

Google Is Born

Google founders Larry Page and Sergey Brin met at Stanford University in 1995. The two men had a lot in common. Both were born in 1973, both were obsessed with computers from an early age, and both were studying for Ph.D.s in computer science.

Google cofounders (Sergey left, Larry right) in their messy office in Mountain View, California in 2002.

When Larry arrived at Stanford, Sergey had already been there for two years and was part of the team that welcomed Larry to the campus. Apparently the pair disagreed on just about everything during that first meeting, but gradually they got to know each other and became good friends.

One night, Larry woke up from a dream with his vision for Google fully formed in his head. "I was thinking: What if we could download the whole Web, and just keep the links? I grabbed a pen and started writing!"

Larry realized that the links between sites — the shortcuts and "road signs" that told you where to go and why — were the result of conscious effort. Internet users were "voting" for the best links whenever they chose to visit a Web site, or when they included a link on their own site. Larry started downloading the entire structure of the Internet — something that Google is still doing today!

Larry's project also caught Sergey's imagination, and the two men became obsessed not just with creating a new search engine, but with creating the

best, most useful, most efficient search engine ever. Their project was first called BackRub (apparently a reference to their mathematical formula, which counts backlinks as votes), but the pair soon changed the name to Google, a common misspelling of "googol," or 10100 — the amount of traffic that they hoped the Web site would one day handle.

> " I realized I wanted to invent things, but I also wanted to change the world. Inventing things isn't enough. You have to get them out into the world and have people use them to have any effect. So probably from when I was 12, I knew I was going to start a company eventually. "
>
> **Larry Page**

Brains Behind the Brand

Larry Page – Cofounder and President, Products
Larry Page was Google's founding Chief Executive Officer (CEO). He grew the company to more than 200 employees and increased profitability before moving into his role as President of Products in April 2001. In April 2011, he took over his original position as Chief Executive Officer, replacing former CEO Eric Schmidt.

A company CEO's main responsibilities are to ensure that all lines of business are running efficiently and within a budget set by the board of directors. The CEO usually works with senior-level managers to devise plans that will generate revenues, create new business opportunities and help the company remain competitive in the marketplace.

← Larry's love of technology began at the age of six, when he became an award-winning junior scientist.

Setting up the Company

Larry and Sergey delivered a paper — an academic study — on Google to their Stanford professors in January 1998. It was called "The Anatomy of a Large-Scale Hypertextual Web Search Engine," and can still be seen at http://infolab.stanford.edu/~backrub/google.html.

This is the first Google headquarters at 232 Santa Margarita, Menlo Park, California.

At first, both men wanted to finish their studies, but eventually decided to take a break from Stanford to found Google and try to make a success of it as a company. They reasoned that

Brains Behind The Brand

Sergey Brin – Cofounder
Sergey was born in Moscow but moved to the USA when he was seven years old. His father was a professor of mathematics at the University of Maryland, and his mother was a scientist at NASA's Goddard Space Flight Center. After graduating from the University of Maryland, Sergey received a National Science Foundation scholarship to study computer science at Stanford.

Sergey cofounded Google in 1998, and directs special projects. While Larry focuses on leading the company, Sergey loves to explore the technology! Among other tasks, Sergey tries to find ways to improve Google Search, making it faster and more accurate than ever.

they would both come back and finish their Ph.D.s if things didn't work out.

In September 1998, Google got its first investment — four investors putting in around $250,000 each. One of the investors was Amazon.com founder Jeff Bezos. Larry and Sergey rented their first office space for $1,700 per month at 232 Santa Margarita Avenue, a double garage and two downstairs spare rooms of a house in Menlo Park, in the Bay Area of California, south of San Francisco.

Their office space consisted of three tables, three chairs, a small fridge, an old washing machine and a table tennis table folded up in the corner because they didn't have the space to play on it.

They kept the garage door open for ventilation and their desks were pine doors resting on trestle tables. On the garage door they put a sign saying "Google Worldwide Headquarters"!

Apart from its initial $1 million investment, Google had a $20,000 per month contract to provide specialized search results to a consulting company. Nevertheless, Larry and Sergey were determined to move quickly and keep growing. At that stage Google had indexed just 10 percent of the Web. By the end of 1998, there were six engineers crammed into the garage, so the company relocated to a bigger space above a bike shop in Palo Alto. A second round of funding followed in June 1999, with an investment of $25 million. That summer, they were up to 40 employees. Google was on its way.

Google's offices in Dublin, Ireland.

Business Matters

Forming a company — A public company is a business owned by shareholders (people who own shares in the company), and run by directors. The company's shares have a $1 market value, which goes up and down depending on how good an investment the shares are judged to be by people outside the company who want to buy those shares.

Sergey has published many academic papers on search engines, is a recipient of a National Science Foundation Graduate Fellowship and has been a featured speaker at several international academic, business and technology events.

Standing out from the Competition

Other search engines at the time like Excite, Lycos and Yahoo! were developing into portals (gateways to larger, more sophisticated Web sites containing general interest content, news and so on), that tried to keep visitors on their sites. Google, however, remained focused on the importance of searches, and providing users with the best possible free service, giving them the answer to their questions and directing them away from Google as quickly as possible.

This focus on simplicity can be seen in the Google homepage. The page loads quickly, and the clean design makes it absolutely clear how to proceed in your search for information. Despite many offers from advertisers who wanted banners on the homepage, Larry and Sergey were determined to have a simple, functional front page without advertising or pictures. They also wanted something that looked very different from other search engines.

The pair hired Ruth Kedar to create Google's distinctive multi-colored logo, which is meant to look, according to Kedar "almost non-designed... The colors evok[ing] memories of child play."

From 1999 to 2000 the number of searches Google was handling rose from 500,000 per day to 7 million. But Larry and Sergey still didn't know how to make money from Google. Their first plan was to charge companies for delivering valuable information from advanced search results. The pair never wavered, however, from their belief that a great search engine would eventually be a huge success.

Gradually, Google got its foot on the corporate ladder. A deal was signed to make Google the default search engine on Web browser Netscape, which meant a huge boost in traffic.

For a long time, Larry and Sergey avoided the idea of ads on the site, worrying it would slow down the searches. In 2000, their revenues were $19.1 million, but their losses were $14.7 million. Google was quickly burning through their cash.

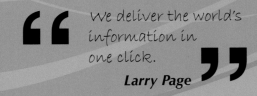
The homepages for Yahoo!, Google and Bing.

> **We deliver the world's information in one click.**
> *Larry Page*

Artist and designer Ruth Kedar is the person responsible for the distinctive Google logo.

Business Matters

Branding — All the qualities and features of a product, including its name and its appearance, are presented to the customer as a brand. To be successful, all brands — from Google to McDonalds to Nike — need to be distinctive (stand out in some way from competitors), consistent (always provide the same level of quality, and therefore be seen as reliable), recognizable (through a logo or "look" of a product) and attractive. Everyone recognizes Google's simple white homepage and multicolored logo!

CHAPTER 6

Making a Profit

By the end of 2000, Google was the most visited search engine on the Web, with one hundred million daily search queries, and a worldwide market share of 40 percent. But it was only with the invention of two products — AdWords and AdSense — that it started to become profitable.

AdWords, introduced in October 2000, allows potential advertisers to bid to place small text ads (the ads you see as "sponsored links" on the right-hand page of a Google search) next to the results for key word searches. American Airlines and Air France might compete for ad space next to keywords like "flights" or "holiday," for example.

All auctions for ads are run online through an automated system. The highest bidder for a keyword gets to place a small text ad that appears at the top of the shaded box to the right of the search results. Up to ten lower bidders also get ad space below the winner.

Google sets the minimum bid per adword — common words like "holiday" might cost one or two cents, while more specialized words like "helicopter parts" might cost several dollars per click.

AdSense is a separate program that brings together Web advertisers with Web sites that want advertising. For example, placing a football jersey manufacturer with a sports news Web site, or a lawyer with a legal advice site. The system is automated and simple — there are no ad sales people, and no bartering over prices.

Google's system — cost per click (CPC) — makes sure that advertisers are only charged when the user clicks on an ad.

▲ *Millions of people search Google to get the best holiday deals.*

In 2008, Google paid out $5 billion to its hundreds of thousands of ad partners while still making a significant profit. Google could now tap into the lucrative Web advertising market and make a profit for the first time. Company profits for 2008 were $4.2 billion on revenues of $21.8 billion. Ninety seven percent of this revenue came from advertising!

Advertisers are provided with an efficient, measurable service. They can count the amount of clicks they receive, and so can decide where they should be spending their money. According to Google, consumers also benefit because they only see ads that are relevant to them.

> Eric is the leader for the company. Larry and Eric and I all share in the top-level leadership, but mostly Eric takes on the hardest challenges. Larry and I spend more time on products and technology.
>
> **Sergey Brin**

▼ *This is an AdSense page.*

Google AdSense

Change Language: English (US

Discover your site's full revenue potential.

Google AdSense is a fast and easy way for website publishers of all sizes to display relevant, unobtrusive Google ads on their website's content pages and earn money. Because the ads are related to what your users are looking for on your site, you'll finally have a way to both monetize and enhance your content pages.

It's also a way for website publishers to provide Google web and site search to their visitors, and to earn money by displaying Google ads on the search results pages.

What is AdSense?
Quick Tour

Getting started is easy!
Click Here to Apply

Brains Behind The Brand

Dr. Eric Schmidt – Executive Chairman (CEO)

Since joining Google in 2001, Eric has helped grow the company from a Silicon Valley start-up to a global enterprise. With founders Sergey Brin and Larry Page, Eric oversaw Google's technical and business strategy. Under Eric's leadership, the company's business has extended far beyond search. One of Eric's roles was to remain "customer focused" — this means he had to make sure that all Google's new products were useful and, most importantly, easy to use. In 2011, he stepped down as CEO and took on the role of Executive Chairman.

Before joining Google, Eric was the Chairman and CEO of Novell, and Chief Technology Officer at Sun Microsystems, Inc., where he led the development of a famous computer program called Java.

CHAPTER 7
Keeping the Staff Happy

Google's continued success is partly based on attracting the best and brightest talents in Silicon Valley, and hanging onto them in the face of competition from other big high-tech companies. One way Google fosters worker satisfaction is through its great working conditions.

The Google office in the Netherlands has its own indoor bike lane.

Brains Behind The Brand

Laszlo Bock – Vice President, People Operations

Laszlo is Google's worldwide head of human resources. It is his job to attract talented people to join Google, provide them with the training and development opportunities they need to keep growing and then keep them from moving to other competing high-tech firms!

Laszlo holds a degree in International Relations from Pomona College, and an MBA from the Yale University School of Management.

Google's HQ in Mountain View, California — known as the Googleplex — is like a huge, luxury estate. It is a collection of two– and three–story buildings with outdoor tables and park benches shaded by trees. There is a vegetable garden and volleyball courts, and bicycles are provided for employees to travel between the buildings.

Staff members are offered free on-site massages and haircuts, pet care facilities and three free healthy meals a day from award-winning chefs. Google spends $70 million every year on free meals and snacks for their employees. Also available are car washes, dry cleaners, vets, gyms, and five doctors' offices offering free medical care. Wi-Fi equipped buses bring employees to and from work, running from early morning to late at night.

Employees all get a free laptop, and most are also given one day per week (20 percent of their time) to work on projects they feel passionately about. The policy obviously works. One employee, Google's principal research scientist Krishna Bharat, invented Google News with his 20 percent time!

Salaries are average, but most employees are offered stock options (shares in Google), meaning that every year, they receive a percentage of the company's profits (known as dividends). In 2008, Google paid out a massive $1.1 billion in dividends, often turning members of staff into millionaires overnight!

Business Matters

Human Resources — The Human Resources (HR) department of a company is responsible for putting in place and maintaining the business practices that allow effective people management. Some key responsibilities of an HR department are: 1) training; 2) staff appraisal: a formal process, performed by managers on their staff, which aims to communicate how they are performing and to discuss what they need in order to improve and develop; 3) staff development: the processes in the company designed to identify the people with potential, keep them in the organization, and move them into the right positions.

Google employees working at the Chicago office.

Not surprisingly, in 2007 and 2008 *Fortune* magazine named Google as the best US company to work for. At the start of 2008, Google employed 20,000 people, and was adding an extra 150 people every week. During the year they received 1,000,000 job applications!

Google Goes Public

Google was expanding, and hired its first CEO, Eric Schmidt, in February 2001. In 2003 the company passed 500 shareholders and US law stated that within a year they had to offer their shares for sale on the stock market, or open their "accounts" (the details of their income and costs) to the public.

Larry and Sergey did not want to sell shares in Google as they preferred to keep the running of the company private, but they decided that was a better option than risk competitors gaining valuable information by looking at their accounts. So on August 19, 2004, Google shares went on sale on the New York Stock Exchange in a process called an IPO (which means "initial public offering").

Investment bankers were hoping for a price of $85 per share, but trading ended on the first day at $100! The stock reached $108.31 the following day, and by January 31, 2005 had jumped to nearly $200.

In the early days of Google, all new employees were offered stock options. This meant they owned part of the company and would make a percentage of the value of the company if and when they ever sold their stock. At the end of the first day's trading more than 900 Google millionaires had been created. Eventually, seven directors — including Larry and Sergey (who owned 32 percent of the company each) and Eric Schmidt (who owned 6.1 percent) — would become billionaires. Larry and Sergey were just 31 years

The NASDAQ welcomes Google to the stock market in 2004.

old but they remained focused on expanding and growing the business. They stressed to all shareholders that the company would not accept money from advertisers for a better search ranking. What's more, underperforming (and therefore less relevant) ads, would drop down to a lower position on the Google search page, and more relevant ads would move up, even if advertisers had paid less for them! The PageRank system — based on usefulness rather than profit — proved that Google was not interested in sacrificing their long-term success or the usefulness of the product for short-term financial gain.

▼ *This graph shows the profit, loss and revenue figures for Google.*

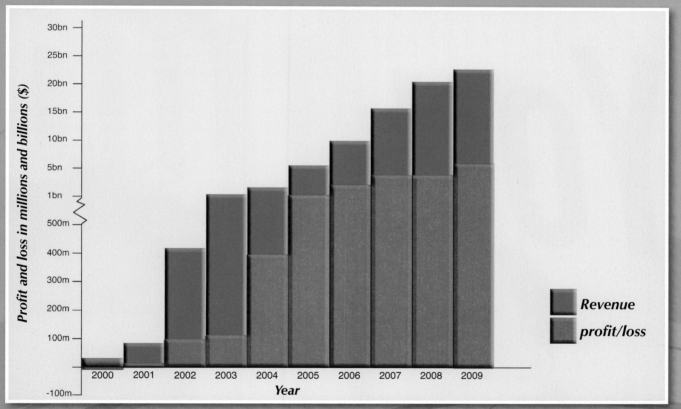

Business Matters

Company shareholders — Shareholders at companies like Google hope to make money in two ways. First, as the company makes money, the value of its shares will rise, so an investor can make a profit if he or she sells their shares (known as a capital gain). Second, part of the profit that a company makes every year can be given to shareholders based on how many shares they own. This is called a dividend.

CHAPTER 9

Expanding the Business

In October 2006, Google bought video-sharing Web site YouTube for a massive $1.65 billion. The media world was stunned. YouTube was attracting 34 million monthly views, and four out of every ten video Web site visitors. But it was making no money!

Business Matters

Market research —
all successful
companies understand
the market in which
they are operating,
and the actions of
their competitors. For
Google, this means
understanding what
the site's users want,
and what other
search engines are in
competition with them.
They watch the market
closely and take note
of any changes. For
example, when people
started spending more
time online through
their mobile phones,
Google launched a
mobile search service.

YouTube founders Chad Hurley and Steve Chen saw Google's offer as a way not only of allowing them to strengthen the video site's technical infrastructure (which was struggling to cope with the huge number of users), but also to help them work out how to get the site to make money.

Chad and Steve built YouTube as a quick and easy way for them to upload and share video clips with their friends. The site soon became somewhere millions of visitors could watch a large selection of user-generated content (UGC) — home videos, clips of pets and events recorded with handheld video cameras. As time went on, though, users started posting music videos, sports clips and shows like *Saturday Night Live* that they had recorded from television.

Chad Hurley and Steve Chen, cofounders of YouTube, attend a news conference in Paris in 2007.

Brains Behind The Brand

Omid Kordestani – Senior Adviser, Office of the CEO and Founders
The first non-engineer to be hired by Google, Omid joined the company in 1999 as senior vice president of global sales and business development. He was directly responsible for the company's worldwide revenue generation, as well as the day-to-day management of the sales team. Omid helped bring Google to profitability in record time, generating more than $10 billion in revenue in 2006. Omid is now focused on identifying new revenue opportunities for Google.

Commercial TV channels attract viewers with programs produced by other companies, and then sell advertising. Google believed it could make YouTube profitable in the same way. The longer people stayed on the site looking at clips, the more pages they would view, and the more page views, the higher the ad rates would become.

But Google still faces several problems before it can make YouTube profitable. First, the Web site doesn't own any clips that appear on it, and only avoids being sued by TV and film companies by immediately removing any content it is asked to take down.

Second, the TV networks, record companies and film studios are demanding large licensing fees to allow YouTube to keep their content on the site. Google has offered a generous split of ad revenues, but there have been only a limited number of agreements, and as late as 2009 YouTube still lost $500 million. Has Google made a costly mistake with YouTube? Only time will tell.

Omid was previously vice president of business development and sales at Internet pioneer Netscape Communications. He grew online revenue from $88 million to more than $200 million in just 18 months.

Diversifying the Business

There's now much more to Google than searches. In this spread we focus on some of Google's other products.

Google TV (http://www.google.com/tv/) — allows you to access the Internet, and a wide range of apps through your home television. Search for your favorite shows and Google TV will find all the content available — from TV shows, to Web clips to apps — and allow you to access it all with just one click!

Google Earth (http://www.google.com/earth/index.html) — launched in 2005, this "virtual globe" provides satellite images from around the world, allowing users to zoom into busy London shopping streets or war-torn Baghdad.

Chrome (http://www.google.com/chrome) — Google's Web browser, released in 2008, provides easy access to all Google's applications. As of October 2010, it had captured 9.71 percent of the Web browser

market, compared to Internet Explorer's 44.72 percent.

Google Maps (http://maps.google.com/) — launched in 2005, this allows users to plan routes and follow map directions by foot, in the car or on public transport.

Google Videos (http://video.google.com/) — this free video sharing Web site and search engine, launched in 2005, has failed to capture a significant share of the online video market, and in 2009 discontinued the ability for users to upload videos.

Google Docs (https://docs.google.com/#all) — launched in 2005, this free, Web-based word processing, presentation and data storage service is extremely popular. It offers "cloud computing"

Google Earth provides satellite images of the planet's nearly 60 million square miles (155 million square kilometer

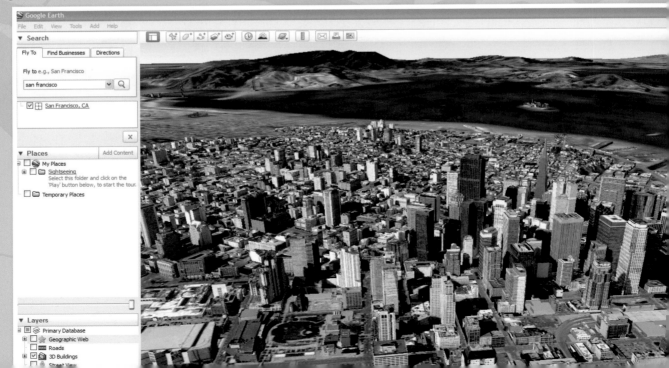

Brains Behind The Brand

Susan Wojcicki – Senior Vice President, Product Management
Susan joined Google in 1999 as the company's first marketing manager. She worked on the initial viral marketing programs to get people talking about and using the search engine. She also led the development of several important products including Google Images, Google Books and Google Video.

Gmail also features instant messaging. ▼

— storing large documents securely on the Internet rather than on your home computer.

Gmail (http://mail.google.com/) — Google's free e-mail service was launched in 2007. Unlike services like Yahoo!, which offer 4Mb of storage, Google offers 1 Gigabyte, 250 times as much.

Google Books (http://books.google.com/) — launched in 2004, this aims to digitize and make searchable every book ever published. Google believes the project will bring back to life out-of-print books, but publishing companies and authors argue that it will damage book sales.

Google eBooks (http://books.google.com/ebooks) — like many companies, Google also launched an eBookstore in late 2010. Downloads can be read on computers, Android and Apple mobile devices, but not on Amazon's Kindle.

Google News (http://news.google.com/) — launched in 2002, this offers free access to content from 25,000 publishers worldwide. It is completely non-biased and independent.

Business Matters

Diversification
— Companies often decide to offer new products or services — like Google Maps and Street View — because it reduces the risk of its other products becoming too limited or uninteresting. By adding new products to its range, Google is providing an extra reason for users to visit the site. When companies offer a completely different product or service, like supermarkets offering car or house insurance, this is called diversification and "brandstretching."

CHAPTER 11
Google Changes the World

Google has helped change the way we all access information. Larry and Sergey's revolutionary search engine appeared at the start of a decade that saw more and more people going online, and the beginning of a dramatic improvement in high-speed Internet access into homes worldwide. Google Search made navigating the Internet much simpler, and in turn increased the number of people searching for resources online. The Internet generation was born.

And the Internet generation, according to author Chris Anderson, who wrote the book *Free: The Future of a Radical Price*, want their information for nothing! So Google, which makes over 90 percent of its income from advertising, can provide the best free access to information resources around the world — and get advertisers to pay for it.

This business model works the same way for commercial television broadcasters. Their programs are funded by the money they receive from brands to advertise their products during commercial breaks. But TV channels are now feeling "the Google effect" — they are losing viewers as more people spend time online, watching video clips on sites like YouTube. Viewing figures are falling, and TV channels are forced to drop their ad rates as a result.

Google's ad system, which allows advertisers to track and monitor every mouse click, is also eating into traditional print advertising. So even though Google Search and Google News are generating more than one billion clicks per month to newspaper Web sites, newspapers are still in danger of closing down because they can't make money from the Internet traffic.

Google employees hold an informal meeting at the Dublin office.

> " [Larry and I] agree 80-90 percent of the time. If we both feel the same way, we're probably right... If we both agree and nobody else agrees with us, we assume we're right! That's sort of what you need to do to make progress. "
>
> *Sergey Brin*

Google has been a big winner from the Internet generation, but they are also aware that nothing lasts forever. Just as traditional media is being replaced by the Internet, even formerly large Internet companies like Lycos, MySpace and Yahoo! have seen their fortunes rise and fall. To maintain its success in ten, 20, even 50 years from now, Google is devoting a lot of time planning for the future.

Brains Behind The Brand

Marissa Mayer – Vice President of Location and Local Services
Marissa joined Google in 1999 as the company's first female engineer. In the last ten years she has worked on internationalizing the Google Web site into more than 100 languages, refining Google News and Gmail and launching more than 100 features and products on Google.com.

Marissa now leads the company's Location and Local Services.

In 2008, at just 33, Marissa became the youngest woman ever to be included on Fortune *magazine's Most Powerful Women list.*

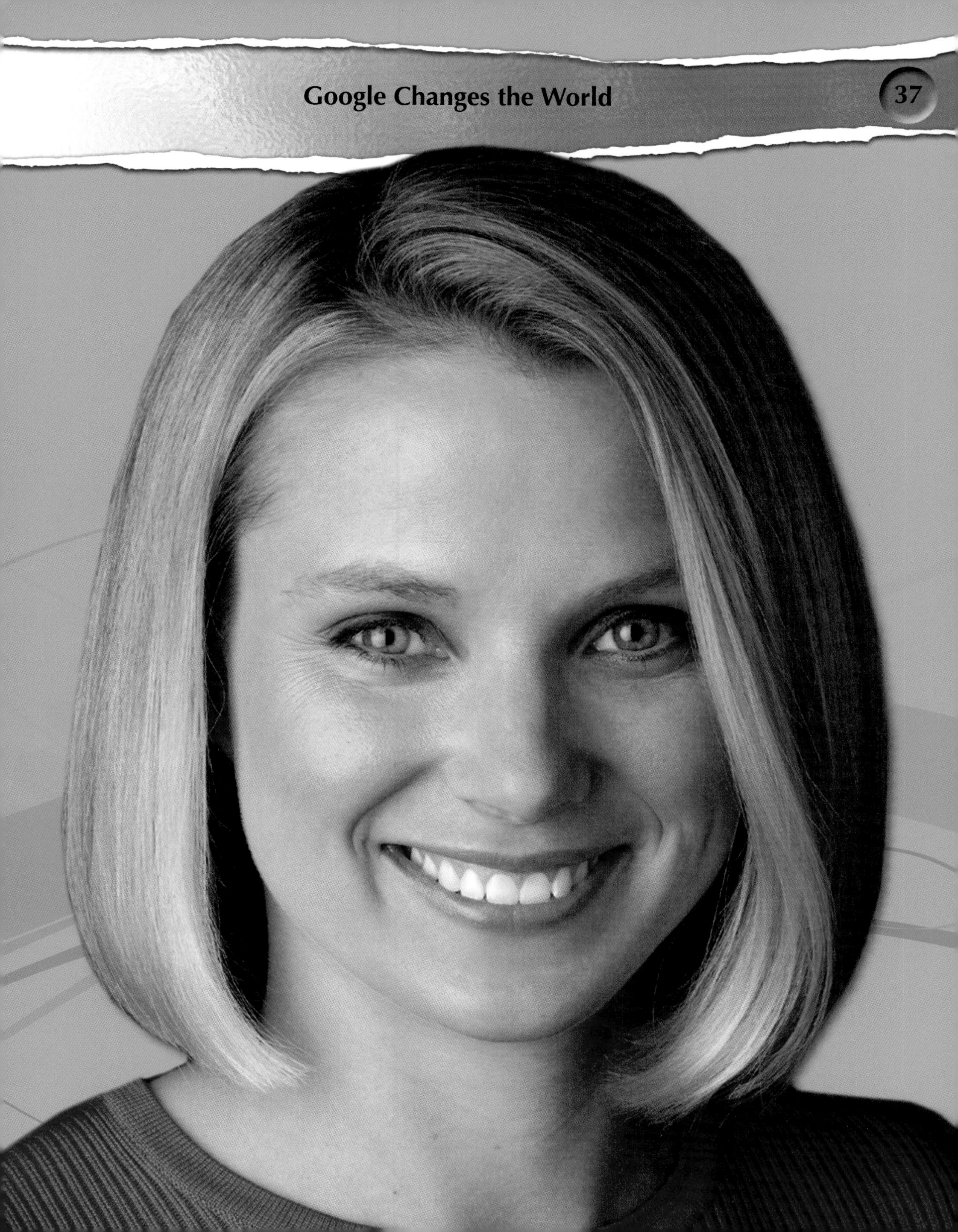

CHAPTER 12

Making Google Future-Proof

Google is also concerned about the environment. This is an overview of the solar panel installation at the Googleplex in California.

Where will Google go from here? Right now, it is the undisputed king of searches, and it is working hard not to stand still.

Brains Behind The Brand

Vinton G. Cerf – Vice President and Chief Internet Evangelist
Widely known as a "Father of the Web," Vinton was the codesigner with Robert Kahn of the TCP/IP software code that is used to transmit data across the Internet. The invention won both men the highest civilian honor bestowed in America, the Presidential Medal of Freedom for "transform[ing] global commerce, communication and entertainment."

Vinton holds a Ph.D. in Computer Science from UCLA and more than a dozen honorary degrees. Hugely experienced and respected around the world, Vinton is responsible for identifying new enabling technologies and applications on the Internet and other platforms for Google. In other words, he's looking for technologies that we will be using in five, ten and twenty years' time.

To survive and prosper in the long term, Google needs to make itself an essential part of our lives, just as Google Search is within its own market. Already, several of Google's products — particularly the e-mail service Gmail, along with Google Maps, Google Earth, Street View and Google Docs — are extremely successful and widely used, but others like Google Videos have failed to match the competition.

So how does Google plan to stay relevant? One way it can grow is by trying to buy success. Like the purchase of YouTube, it could use its considerable funds to buy into other successful businesses. It was outbid by Microsoft when Facebook sold 1.6 percent of its shares in October 2007, but there will no doubt be other purchases that see Google growing into new, unexpected areas.

Like all successful companies, Google is facing competition, most significantly from software giant Microsoft. The huge computer company is heavily promoting its own search engine, Bing, which launched in May 2009 and merged with the established Yahoo! brand in July 2009. So far, Bing is a long way behind Google's search numbers but it trying hard to increase its share of the search market and the advertising revenues that go with it.

Google has always been known for product innovation, and the quality of its search, and it reinforced those qualities with the launch in 2010 of Google Instant. The new, improved search promises to deliver results before you have even finished typing!

What's more, Google will continue to focus on boosting its revenue from advertising sales, and hope to increase its dominance of the online advertising market. In April 2007 it bought DoubleClick, a company that allows Web sites to sell online ads, and advertisers and ad agencies to buy them. Google plans to be around for many, many years to come.

Google can be accessed directly on iPads and smartphones.

> We began as a technology company, and have evolved into a software, technology, internet, advertising and media company all rolled into one.
>
> *Eric Schmidt*

To create a new product, it is helpful to put together a product development brief like the one below. This is a sample brief for Google TV.

SWOT analysis on the page opposite can help you to think about the strengths, weaknesses, opportunities and threats of your product. This can let you to see how feasible and practical your idea is before you think of investing in it.

Product Development Brief

Name of product: Google TV

Type of product: A searchable archive of TV shows from around the world, sourced from archives.

The product explained (use 25 words or less): TV lovers — you never need to leave your computer to watch your favorite programs from around the world. Any program at any time!

Target age of users: 1-100

What does the product do? The product allows Google users to access archived TV shows from around the world. Google TV stores every episode of every show with partner TV channels, allowing viewers to catch up on any episodes they have missed. The shows can run with new Google-placed ads in them to maximize revenue for Google.

What makes your product different? TV viewers who want to catch up on their favorite programs currently have to visit individual websites but this product will put the content from all of these sites into one place, and make them easily searchable and watchable. It will become the one-stop shop for TV addicts around the world!

Name of Google product you are assessing ... Google TV
The table below will help you assess your Google product. By addressing all four areas, you can make your application stronger, and more likely to be a success.

Questions to consider

Does your product do something unique?

Is there anything innovative about it?

Does it have any additional uses?

What are its USPs (unique selling points)?

Strengths

No other similar products currently available.

It's USP is that it brings every television program in the world onto your computer, and allows you to search them!

Why wouldn't people use this product?

How many channels are currently available to access?

Does it do everything it says it can?

Does it work on all kinds of computers — PCs and Macs?

Weaknesses

People might prefer spending time sitting comfortably in their living rooms watching television.

The product at the moment can only access the program that each television broadcaster makes available. This means it is limited.

Will the issue that the product tackles become more important over time?

Will new markets emerge for this product?

Can the product target new 'niche' (i.e. small, specific) markets?

Can it be used globally?

Can it develop new USPs?

Opportunities

People will become more "time poor" — in other words, their free time will get less, and therefore more important to them, so this product will become more important.

More and more TV channels will create archives for their TV shows, so the product will have more and more content as time goes on.

Can be used around the world.

Is the market (i.e. Google traffic) shrinking?
Are people moving to other search engines?

Will new technology make your product unnecessary?

Are any of your weaknesses so bad they might affect the application in the long run?

Will competitors produce a better product?

Threats

Google traffic is still strong and growing, but there will definitely be other search engines trying to compete.

A TV broadcaster like Sky or Virgin in the UK might be able to produce a similar service.

Do You Have What It Takes to Work at Google? Try This!

1) You have a math homework question you don't understand. Do you:

a) Leave it. You'll ask the teacher tomorrow.

b) Ask your mom, then write down anything, just to get it finished.

c) Go online and research it. You're not going to let one question beat you!

2) You have a presentation to do at school. Do you:

a) Not prepare. You always think better on your feet.

b) Jot down some notes off the top of your head. You'll look at them to remind you.

c) Spend a week preparing handouts for your classmates, and a Powerpoint presentation to show on the pull-down screen in the classroom.

3) You're given a Rubik's Cube as a present. Do you:

a) Leave it in a box under your bed.

b) Have a go at solving it, but get stuck after doing one side.

c) Solve it in half an hour, then start working on designing a better Rubik's Cube.

4) It's coming up to your exams. Do you:

a) Not worry about it. You're going to work for your dad anyway.

b) Get all the text books out and read through your work until you get bored.

c) Prepare detailed revision timetables and produce notes on each subject. You want all A's!

5) You're given a computer for your birthday. Do you:

a) Use it for Facebook and watching YouTube

b) Use it for homework, e-mail, Facebook and watching YouTube

c) Take out the motherboard and reconfigure it to make it faster and more efficient.

6) Your hero is:

a) Peter Kay — he's the funniest comedian in the country.

b) Nelson Mandela — he fought for what he believed in, and ended Apartheid in South Africa.

c) Nikola Tesla — his work led to the development of electricity, X-rays and wireless communication.

Results

Mostly As: Sorry, but your chance of working at Google is looking shaky! It doesn't sound like you have the interest in computers to succeed at this world-famous company.

Mostly Bs: You are thoughtful and hard-working, but you need to work on standing out from the pack if you want to succeed in a very competitive business.

Mostly Cs: It sounds like you might have what it takes to get a job at Google! Keep working hard at school, and pushing to be the best.

Glossary

app Short for application. An app is computer software that helps the user perform a task.

barter To negotiate or haggle over the price of something.

Chief Internet Evangelist Google's own made-up term for Vinton Cerf. An evangelist is someone who preaches or spreads the word, usually of God, in order to make people into believers. In Vinton's case, he spreads the word on the Internet to make people believe in its potential.

corporate Relating to the structure and organization of a company.

digitize To turn a physical product, like a book, into a digital version that can be read on computers.

discontinue To stop producing something.

distinctive Recognizable; eye-catching.

diversify To vary products and services in order to expand or to spread risk.

efficient Working in the most effective way with the least waste of time or resources.

enterprise Another word for a company.

foster To promote or encourage.

founding a company To start or launch a company.

functional Practical; working efficiently without problems.

graduate To receive a university degree.

infrastructure The basic structure of a company; how it is organized into departments.

lucrative Profitable.

market share The percentage of a market that a company controls.

obsessed Focused completely on something or someone.

PC Short for personal computer.

phenomenon A remarkable or outstanding occurrence.

portal An entrance or gateway (in this case, to a larger internet site).

post To put information online.

query A question.

reinforce To stress; give added strength or support to something.

reputable Trustworthy; having a good reputation; respectable.

revenue A company's income before costs are taken into account; gross income.

search engine A Web site designed to find Internet links that match your search.

Silicon Valley Region in the San Francisco Bay Area of Northern California. It is home to many of the world's largest technology corporations.

Street View A feature in Google Maps and Google Earth that provides views from various positions along many streets in the world.

waver To hesitate or be unsure about something.

unique One of a kind; unequalled.

For More Information

Google, Inc.

1600 Amphitheatre Parkway

Mountain View, CA 94043

(650) 253-0000

Web site: http://www.google.com

The most popular search engine in the world, Google now extends its line of products to systems that are designed to "organize the world's information."

Microsoft

One Microsoft Way

Redmond, WA 98052-6399

(800) Microsoft

Web site: http://www.microsoft.com

Microsoft is the world's leading software maker and had recently faced tough competition with Web-based tech companies such as Google and Yahoo!.

Search Engine Marketing Professional Organization (SEMPO)

401 Edgewater Place, Suite 600

Wakefield, MA 01880

(781) 876-8866

Web site: http://www.sempo.org

SEMPRO is the global, non-profit association for search marketing professionals.

SeoPros

3608 Dufferin Street, Suite #1

Toronto, ON M3K 1N7

Canada

(416) 638-4148

Web site: http://www.seopros.org/

SeoPros is one of the leading organizations of search optimization professionals.

Yahoo!

701 First Avenue

Sunnyvale, CA 94089

(408) 349-3300

Web site: http://www.yahoo.com

Yahoo! is one of the world's largest search engines and a leading Internet community, providing games, e-mail and other Web services to users.

Web Sites

Due to the changing nature of Internet links, Rosen Publishing has developed an online list of Web sites related to the subject of this book. This site is updated regularly. Please use this link to access the list:

http://www.rosenlinks.com/bht/goo

Anderson, Chris. *The Long Tail: Why the Future of Business Is Selling Less of More*. New York, NY: Hyperion, 2008.

Auletta, Ken. *Googled: the End of the World as We Know It*. New York, NY: Penguin, 2010.

Battelle, John. *The Search: How Google and Its Rivals Rewrote the Rules of Business and Transformed Our Culture*. New York, NY: Portfolio, 2006.

Carr, Nicholas G. *The Big Switch: Rewiring the World, from Edison to Google*. New York, NY: W.W. Norton & Co., 2009.

Conner, Nancy. *Google Apps: the Missing Manual*. New York, NY: O'Reilly, 2008.

Edwards, Douglas. *I'm Feeling Lucky: the Confessions of Google Employee Number 59*. Boston, MA: Houghton Mifflin Harcourt, 2011.

Fox, Vanessa. *Marketing in the Age of Google: a Non-technical Guide to Search Engine Strategy*. Hoboken, NJ: John Wiley & Sons, 2010.

Gilbert, Sara. *The Story of Google*. Collingwood, ON: Saunders Book, 2009.

Girard, Bernard. *The Google Way: How One Company Is Revolutionizing Management as We Know It*. San Francisco, CA: No Starch, 2009.

Hamen, Susan E. *Google: the Company and Its Founders*. Edina, MN: ABDO Publishing, 2011.

Jarvis, Jeff. *What Would Google Do?* New York, NY: HarperCollins, 2009.

Levin, Judith. *Careers Creating Search Engines*. New York, NY: Rosen Pub., 2007.

Levy, Steven. *Hackers* [Heroes of the Computer Revolution]. Beijing, China: O'Reilly, 2010.

Levy, Steven. *In the Plex: How Google Thinks, Works, and Shapes Our Lives*. New York, NY: Simon & Schuster, 2011.

Lowe, Janet. *Google Speaks: Secrets of the World's Greatest Billionaire Entrepreneurs, Sergey Brin and Larry Page*. Hoboken, NJ: John Wiley & Sons, 2009.

Marshall, Perry S., and Bryan Todd. *Entrepreneur Magazine's Ultimate Guide to Google AdWords: How to Access 100 Million People in 10 Minutes*. Irvine, CA: Entrepreneur, 2010.

McPherson, Stephanie Sammartino. *Sergey Brin and Larry Page: Founders of Google*. Minneapolis, MN: Twenty-First Century, 2011.

Tapscott, Don. *Grown up Digital: How the Net Generation Is Changing Your World*. New York, NY: McGraw-Hill, 2009.

Vaidhyanathan, Siva. *The Googlization of Everything: (and Why We Should Worry)*. Berkeley, CA: University of California Press, 2011.

Google